THE ORION SPACECRAFT

Into Deep Space

Diane Bailey

Lerner Publications ◆ Minneapolis

Lerner Publications Company
An imprint of Lerner Publishing Group, Inc.
241 First Avenue North
Minneapolis, MN 55401 USA

For reading levels and more information, look up this title at www.lernerbooks.com.

Main body text set in Aptifer Sans Regular.
Typeface provided by Linotype.

Library of Congress Cataloging-in-Publication Data

Names: Bailey, Diane, 1966–author.
Title: The Orion Spacecraft : into deep space / Diane Bailey.
Description: Minneapolis : Lerner Publications, [2024] | Series: Space explorer guidebooks.
    Alternator books | Includes bibliographical references and index. | Audience: Ages 8–12 |
    Audience: Grades 4–6 | Summary: "The Orion Spacecraft might be the key to the future of
    human space travel. Not only could it take us back to the moon, but also to Mars. See why
    Orion is ready for take-off"—Provided by publisher.
Identifiers: LCCN 2023011313 (print) | LCCN 2023011314 (ebook) | ISBN 9798765609071 (library
    binding) | ISBN 9798765624920 (paperback) | ISBN 9798765617908 (epub)
Subjects: LCSH: Orion spacecraft—Juvenile literature. | Manned space flight—Juvenile
    literature. | Space vehicles—United States—Juvenile literature. | BISAC: JUVENILE
    NONFICTION / Science & Nature / Astronomy
Classification: LCC TL789.8.U6 O753 2024 (print) | LCC TL789.8.U6 (ebook) | DDC 629.4500973—
    dc23/eng/20230413

LC record available at https://lccn.loc.gov/2023011313
LC ebook record available at https://lccn.loc.gov/2023011314

Manufactured in the United States of America
1 – CG – 12/15/23

TABLE OF CONTENTS

Commander Moonikin Campos was part of the Artemis 1 uncrewed test flight.

ORION'S FIRST PASSENGER

On November 29, 2022, a man named Moonikin was more than 268,000 miles (431,304 km) away from Earth. That was farther than anyone had ever been before. Moonikin wasn't actually alive. He was a mannequin, or a model of a human. But he had an important job. He was riding on Orion, a new spacecraft built to take humans into deep space. Moonikin's flight would help scientists make sure Orion was safe for real humans. Moonikin spent three and a half weeks in space and then landed safely back on Earth. Orion had passed its first big test!

Moonikin rode in the Orion space capsule around the moon and back. The journey took twenty-five and a half days.

CHAPTER 1

BEFORE ORION

Just weeks after the Soviet Union put the first human in space, NASA astronaut Alan Shepard was launched into orbit aboard Freedom 7.

On May 25, 1961, President John F. Kennedy shared his goal to put the first man on the moon by the end of the decade.

Humans have always been curious about outer space. What is up there? Could people ever go? In the 1950s, the United States and the Soviet Union competed to be the first country to get there. The Soviet Union won this "space race" in 1961, when it launched the first cosmonaut into space—for about two hours.

The United States quickly caught up. Just three weeks later, the National Aeronautics and Space Administration (NASA) successfully launched astronaut Alan Shepard into space on the spacecraft Freedom 7. Over the next few years, NASA improved its space travel, using larger, more powerful rockets.

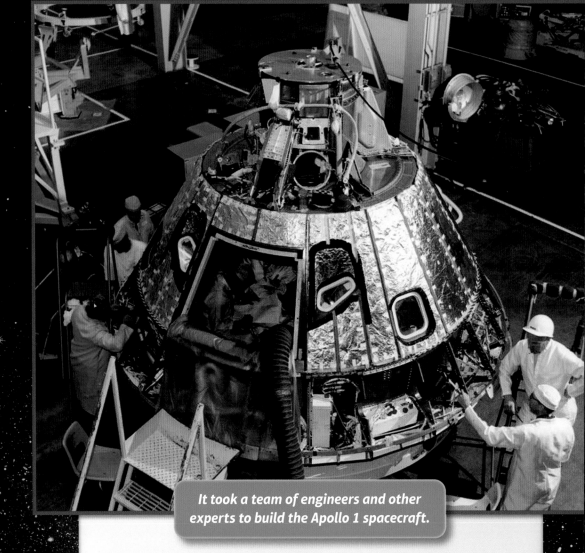

It took a team of engineers and other experts to build the Apollo 1 spacecraft.

MOON MISSIONS

NASA's successes made it confident it could do even more. With the Apollo program in the 1960s, NASA's goal was to reach the moon. The Apollo program had a rocky start. In 1967, a fire on the launchpad killed three astronauts. The program was put on hold while NASA figured out how to make things safer.

The next mission with astronauts was Apollo 11. Everything went smoothly, and on July 20, 1969, Neil Armstrong and Buzz Aldrin became the first humans to walk on the moon. Several more Apollo missions followed before the program ended in 1972. But NASA wasn't quitting space. It was busy working on the next big thing: the space shuttle.

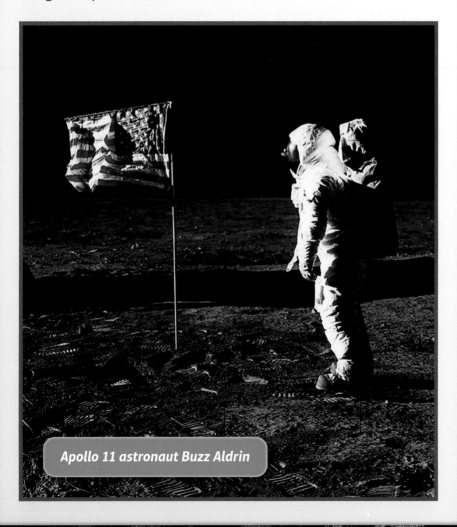

Apollo 11 astronaut Buzz Aldrin

THE SPACE SHUTTLE

The space shuttle was designed to expand people's work in space. It carried satellites into orbit and took people and equipment to space stations. The shuttle program was mostly successful, but there were some tragic accidents. Challenger exploded shortly after lifting off in 1986. In 2003, Columbia broke apart as it reentered Earth's atmosphere after a mission. All the astronauts onboard both spacecrafts were killed. They were proof that human space travel is still difficult and risky.

In the 2000s, the US government decided to end the space shuttle program. It was expensive, and there were other vehicles that could travel to space stations. Plus, NASA had its eye on returning to the moon. The space shuttle wasn't designed to fly into deep space, so NASA needed a brand-new spacecraft. The idea for Orion was born.

NASA's first reusable spacecraft, Space Shuttle Columbia, was launched on April 12, 1981.

All seven members of the Space Shuttle Challenger were lost on the morning of January 28, 1986, just seventy-three seconds after launch.

NOT-SO-HEAVY STUFF

A space station is a laboratory in space. The International Space Station (ISS) is the world's largest. It has a microgravity environment. That means unless they are held down, people and things onboard will float as if they are weightless. The human body is used to working in gravity, so microgravity can mess it up. Bones and muscles get weaker. Vision and hearing can be damaged. The ISS is a good place to observe how the body reacts to microgravity. The results can help scientists develop ways to keep astronauts healthy on future missions.

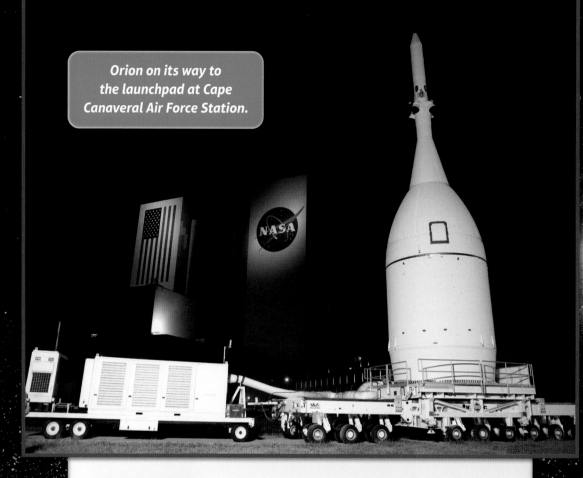

Orion on its way to the launchpad at Cape Canaveral Air Force Station.

CHAPTER 2

BUILDING ORION

Orion is the only spacecraft in the world that's built to take humans into deep space. Deep space refers to areas that are beyond Earth's orbit. This includes trips to the moon, asteroids, and even other planets, like Mars.

LaShawn Boulware

LaShawn Boulware watched the Apollo 13 movie when she was in middle school. It inspired her to become an engineer and to work in human spaceflight. Now, she's a human factors design engineer working on the Orion spacecraft. Her job is to work with the design engineers to ensure that they design with the astronauts' needs in mind. She also works with the astronauts to test everything they'll touch on the spacecraft, from the computer screens to the toilet. She works to make sure things are safe, comfortable, and easy to use.

LaShawn Boulware worked to make the Orion crew module as comfortable as possible.

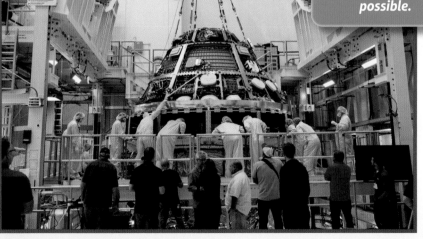

A MODULAR SYSTEM

If you look at the Apollo spacecraft and Orion side-by-side, they seem a lot alike. The gumdrop shape of the Apollo capsules was a good one, and it is the basis for Orion. But there have been a lot of improvements in fifty years. Orion is bigger, safer, and more powerful.

Orion has three main sections. The crew module is sometimes called the capsule. That's where the astronauts live and work. This section of Orion is even reusable. When a spacecraft returns to Earth and lands in the ocean, the saltwater can damage high-tech electronic systems, so most spacecraft are only used once. However, scientists wanted to build Orion so that it could be used many times. They put many of its delicate parts inside the crew module, where the astronauts are. They will stay protected during reentry and can be used again in the future.

The Orion space capsule has enough room for four astronauts and lots of technology.

The service module carries the spacecraft's engines, fuel, and power systems. It also stores water and oxygen for the astronauts. Orion is built so that it can connect to a larger station to get extra power and supplies, but it has enough by itself to support its crew for three weeks without any backup.

The Orion crew module sits on top of its service module.

The Launch Abort System is being installed on the Orion spacecraft.

Finally, there's the launch abort system (LAS). Orion will sit on top of a large rocket that boosts it into space. If something goes wrong, the LAS automatically separates the crew module from the rocket. That helps keep the astronauts safe.

Every detail in the Orion cockpit is carefully designed to make it easy for astronauts to use.

BIGGER AND BETTER

The inside of Orion is filled with the latest technology. Many controls are on glass displays, which saves room that once was filled up with switches and dials. Solar panels generate electricity, so Orion won't have to carry heavy tanks of fuel.

The world's largest heat shield coats the bottom of the capsule. When Orion returns to Earth, it rushes through the atmosphere at 25,000 miles (40,233 km) per hour. That speed creates a lot of friction and heat. The temperature outside the spacecraft reaches about 5,000°F (2,760°C). That's half as hot as the surface of the Sun! The heat shield stops the craft from burning up. Inside, the temperature stays in the mid-70s°F (low-20s°C).

Orion's heat shield protects the capsule and the astronauts inside from intense temperatures when it reenters Earth's atmosphere.

Orion is shaped differently, but it has about the same amount of living space as the inside of a four-door car. Equipment is built into the walls, and supplies are stored in the service module to create as much space as possible in the capsule.

Orion's crew module includes a Universal Waste Management System space toilet.

THE ULTIMATE SUNSCREEN

The Sun emits radiation, which is dangerous to humans. On Earth, the atmosphere protects us. There's no atmosphere in space, so Orion was built to protect its passengers from the radiation. If Orion travels through an area where radiation is especially bad, the astronauts will take shelter in small bunkers built into the floor. They will also surround themselves with storage bags. These extra layers help stop radiation from getting through.

Artemis 2 astronauts will live, work, exercise, and sleep inside the Orion space capsule.

There is enough room for four astronauts. Everyone gets their own chair, which fold up if they're not being used. Sleeping bags hang on the walls. There's also an exercise station, and a small galley to get a drink of water and warm up meals. Orion even has a real toilet. When the Apollo astronauts needed to go to the bathroom, they had to use diapers and bags. A private toilet is a nice improvement!

NASA's Space Launch System rocket carried the Orion spacecraft on top when it launched on November 16, 2022 for the Artemis 1 flight test.

CHAPTER 3

RELYING ON ORION

The first astronauts on the moon did not do much scientific research beyond bringing some moon rocks home to study. This time, NASA wants to do a lot more. Is there ice on the moon? Are there valuable minerals? Scientists want to find out. NASA's new moon program is called Artemis. Orion is key to making it work.

STRESS TEST

NASA spent years designing and testing all of Orion's parts and systems. In November 2022, it was ready for the Artemis 1 mission. This was its biggest test so far. Artemis 1 did not have a human crew, but Orion would have to perform as if it did.

Could Orion do everything it was supposed to? Could it do more? NASA planned to stress it to the limit.

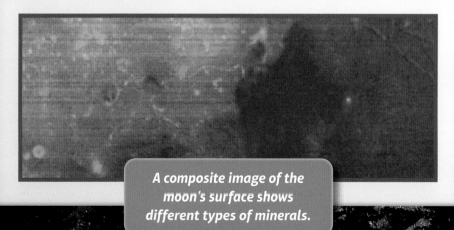

A composite image of the moon's surface shows different types of minerals.

Orion stayed in space for twenty-five days. It traveled 1.4 million miles (2.3 million km), past the moon and back. The mission tested its power, mapping, life support, and communications systems. Everything worked. Moonikin was covered in sensors to test radiation levels. His seat measured how much vibration and acceleration real astronauts would feel.

When Orion returned home, NASA did a skip reentry.

That means it did not plunge straight back to Earth. Instead, it barely hit the outer edge of the atmosphere, and then bounced back up. It looked like a pebble skipping on the surface of a pond. This helped to slow the spacecraft down and gave it time to calculate a more precise landing spot. Splashdown in the Pacific Ocean came on December 11, 2022. Orion's first big mission was a success.

After splashdown, NASA's Orion spacecraft waits for the USS Anchorage to take it home after a flight test.

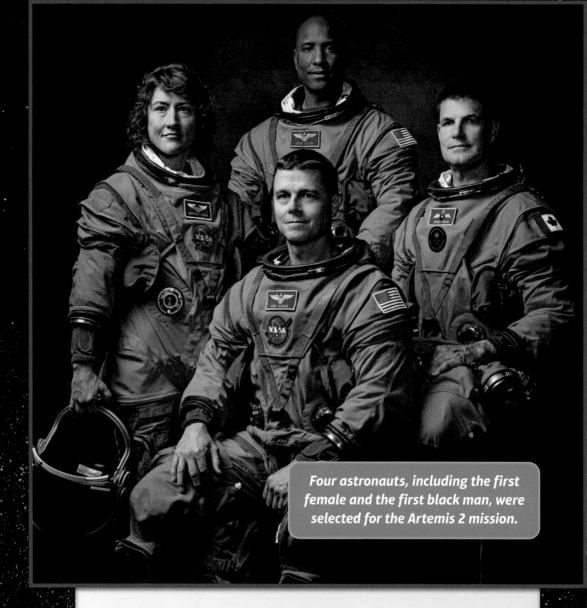

Four astronauts, including the first female and the first black man, were selected for the Artemis 2 mission.

BACK TO THE MOON

Next up is Artemis 2, another mission that will take live astronauts on a ten-day trip around the moon and back. If all goes well, Artemis 3 will land humans on the moon for the first time since 1972. Astronauts will fly Orion into lunar orbit. From there, they will transfer onto a lunar lander that takes them to the moon's surface. Orion will wait for them in orbit. Those astronauts will include the first woman and the first person of color to walk on the moon.

For Artemis 5, NASA will begin building the Lunar Gateway, a space station that will orbit the moon. It will be the headquarters for building a permanent station on the moon's surface. All that will mean transporting a lot of astronauts and supplies. Orion will be kept very busy!

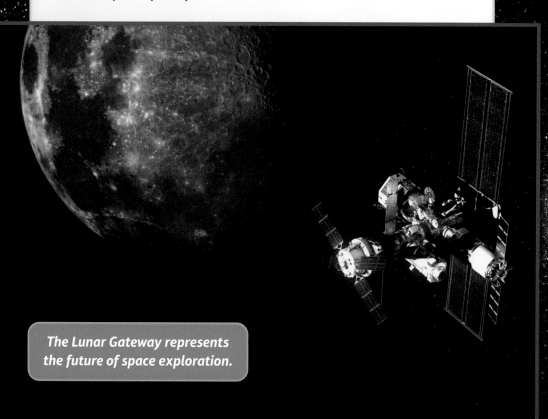

The Lunar Gateway represents the future of space exploration.

GOING DEEPER

In the late 2030s, NASA hopes to send astronauts to Mars. Mars is about 140 million miles (225 million km) away. It will take about nine months to get there, and another nine months to get back to Earth. In between, astronauts will have to wait a few months while the planets line up to make the trip home shorter. Fortunately, that will give them time to study Mars. The whole trip will take a little less than two years.

Orion is too small and does not have enough power to go to Mars by itself. For that, astronauts will use the Deep Space Transport (DST), which NASA is still designing. The DST will

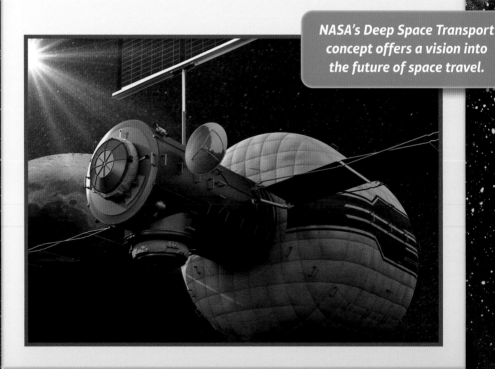

NASA's Deep Space Transport concept offers a vision into the future of space travel.

Mars is high on NASA's priority list for space exploration.

provide more power and room to work. Astronauts could live on it for about three years. The DST would not take off directly from Earth. It would launch from the Lunar Gateway. Orion would take astronauts on the first leg of the journey, to the Lunar Gateway. It's possible Orion might even connect to the DST and go on to Mars. It would then act as a support module for extra computing power and space to work.

NASA wants to use Orion for years to come. It can be our launchpad for space travel, ready to help us explore the solar system.

GLOSSARY

asteroid: a rocky object that orbits the Sun

cosmonaut: an astronaut from the Soviet Union

friction: the resistance that happens when two objects rub against each other

galley: a kitchen

microgravity: an environment that makes people or things seem to be weightless

module: one of several parts that make up a larger object

orbit: the repeating path of an object in space moving around another object

radiation: a type of energy that is dangerous to humans

Soviet Union: a powerful group of Communist states, including Russia, Belarus, Ukraine, Georgia, and eleven others in Europe and Asia, that united from 1922 to 1991 to form one nation

splashdown: when a spacecraft lands in the ocean

LEARN MORE

Betts, Bruce. *Space Exploration for Kids: A Junior Scientist's Guide to Astronauts, Rockets, and Life in Zero Gravity.* Emeryville, CA: Rockridge Press, 2020.

History of Space Travel
https://kids.nationalgeographic.com/space/article/history-of-space-travel

Jackson, Libby. *Space Explorers.* New York: Beyond Words/Aladdin, 2020.

Mara, Wil. *Breakthroughs in Space Travel.* Minneapolis: Lerner Publications, 2019.

NASA Knows: For Students
https://www.nasa.gov/audience/forstudents/5-8/features/nasa-knows/index.html

Orion (Spacecraft) Facts for Kids
https://kids.kiddle.co/Orion_(spacecraft)

Space Place
https://spaceplace.nasa.gov

Swanson, Jennifer. *Spacecare: A Kid's Guide to Surviving Space.* Rochester: Mayo Clinic Press, 2024.

INDEX

PHOTO ACKNOWLEDGMENTS

Page 4; NASA/Ben Smegelsky, page 5; NASA, page 6; NASA, page 7; NASA; page 8; NASA, page 9; NASA; page 10; NASA, page 11; NASA, page 12; NASA/Frankie Martin, page 13; NASA, page 14; Shutterstock/ Dima Zel, page 15; NASA/Robert Markowitz, page 16; NASA/Rad Sinyak, page 17; NASA, page 18; NASA/Radislav Sinyak, page 19; NASA/Isaac Watson, page 20; NASA, page 21; NASA/Joel Kowsky, page 22; NASA/Joel Kowsky, page 23; NASA; 24-25; US Navy, page 26; NASA/James Blair, page 27; NASA, page 28; NASA, page 29; Shutterstock/ Vadim Sadovski.

Cover (image): iStock photo/ dima_Zel
Cover (background): Shutterstock/Maria Starovoytova
Interior background: Shuttesrstock/Sergey Nivens